THE MACMILLAN CONCISE THESAURUS

GORDON PEMBERTON

M
MACMILLAN
EDUCATION

First published 1987

Published by
MACMILLAN EDUCATION LTD
Houndmills, Basingstoke, Hampshire RG21 2XS
and London
Companies and representatives
throughout the world

Printed in Hong Kong

British Library Cataloguing in Publication Data

Pemberton, Gordon
The Macmillan concise thesaurus: the word you want.
1. English language — Synonyms and antonyms
I. Title
423'.1 PE1591

ISBN 0-333-41694-5

Contents

To parents and teachers

This thesaurus is intended for children who already have a writing vocabulary capable of covering most of the subjects they wish to write about. Their most important need is to find alternatives to many of the words they use frequently, so as to avoid repetition of the more common words.

In the main part of this book there are 841 common words. Each word is provided with a list of synonyms (or near-synonyms) from which children can select alternatives for use in their written work.

The list of synonyms for each of the common words contains some that will undoubtedly be already in a child's vocabulary. In such cases the lists will jog the memory. In most cases, however, additional synonyms have been given which would be on the periphery of the child's vocabulary. The purpose of including such synonyms, which are less well-known, is to stretch children into using them. For instance, the common word **delighted** is given the synonyms:

pleased
happy
overjoyed
thrilled
jubilant
ecstatic

The first four of these are probably in the vocabularies of most children. The presence of the last two synonyms may stimulate some of them into making opportunities for their use.

Where appropriate, the opposite of the main word (its antonym) has been given, so that it may be stored in the memory and become available when needed.

Where relevant, the list of synonyms after the main word is followed by irregular or related forms of that word, which may be useful, especially in matters of spelling. For instance, the word **bury** is followed by *buried* because of the changed form of spelling in the past participle. Again, the word **chase** is followed by *chasing*, showing the loss of the letter 'e' in the present participle. There are many examples of this kind.

In the main part of the book the synonym sections include, wherever possible, cross-references to related words referred to by numbers, so as to give the greatest range of synonyms or associated words. For instance, the word **call** has cross-references to the words **cry** and **scream**.

The index contains every word listed in the book (over 7500) with the main words in bold type. The numbers after each word refer to the sections in which it can be found in the main part, thus considerably extending the scope of the book. The number in bold type indicates its main entry.

How to use this book

The contents

This book is arranged in two parts. The main part is the THESAURUS, a list of common words which you often use, called main words. They are arranged alphabetically and are numbered. Each main word is followed by a collection of synonyms (words which mean the same or nearly the same).

The other part of the book is the INDEX. This is a list of all the words used in the book, both main words and synonyms, in alphabetical order, and gives the number of every section in which the word appears. Main words and their section numbers are shown in **bold type**. The numbers of other sections in which the same word appears are shown in ordinary type.

How to find the word you want

The purpose of this book is to help you find the best words to use when you are writing. It also gives you some new words so that you do not have to use the same words again and again. For instance, suppose that you want another word that means *bad*, but you cannot think of one. Look in the main part of the book and find the word *bad*. Under it you will find other words to choose from, all of which mean *bad* or something like it.

Alternatively, look in the index. There you will find **bad** in bold type, followed by the number **47**, also in bold type. Look in the main part of the book under section **47** and you will find the list of synonyms for **bad**.

Suppose that you are looking for a word instead of *alter*. If you cannot find *alter* among the main words, look in the index. There you will find it, followed by its section number, 103. Find section 103 in the main part of the book and you will find other words like *alter* under the main word **change**.

Sometimes you may need a word which means the opposite to one that you have used. In this case, first find the word you have used in the main part of the book or look up its section number in the index. If the word has an opposite you will find it in brackets under the main word.

For example, if you want the opposite to the word *certain*, look it up in the index. You will find that the section number of **certain** is **101**. When you look up that section in the main part of the book you will find the opposite (the antonym) *doubtful* under the word **certain**. It is in brackets to show that it has an opposite meaning. All such antonyms are listed in the index.

This book helps you with unusual spellings of different forms of the main words. These spellings are shown in *italics* at the end of the list of synonyms. For example, other forms of the word **decide** (section **166**) are *deciding* and *decision*. These words, too, are listed in the index.

There are cross-references to help you. For example, at the bottom of the list for the word **chief** (section **109**) you will see the numbers 73 and 92. Look at these sections and you will find the main words **boss** and **captain**. In each of these sections are further words which may help you if you are looking for a word which has a meaning similar to that of **chief**.

THESAURUS

1

able
(unable)

skilful
capable
efficient
experienced
talented
qualified
ability
ably

2

accept
(refuse)

get
take
receive
gain
acquire
secure
acceptable
[see 251, 717]

3

accident
(purpose)

crash
smash
mishap
wreck
tragedy
disaster
accidental
accidentally
[see 151]

4

accuse
(defend)

blame
taunt
summon
denounce
censure
incriminate
accusation

5

across
(along)

crosswise
astride
opposite
beyond
athwart
transverse

6

act

play
perform
portray
pretend
fake
sham
acting
action
active
activity

7

add
(subtract)

count
sum
total
reckon
calculate
compute
addition

8

admire
(despise)

like
love
respect
approve
esteem
venerate
admirable
admiration

9

adult
(child)

man
woman
grown-up
lady
gentleman
person
adulthood

10

adventure

risk
chance
danger
peril
exploit
hazard
adventurous

11

advice

hint
idea
suggestion
guidance
opinion
wisdom
advisable
adviser
[see 12, 312]

12

advise
(deter)

suggest
guide
instruct
persuade
recommend
counsel
advisory
[see 11, 705]

13

afraid
(bold)

scared
frightened
alarmed
worried
nervous
terrified
[see 239]

14

after
(before)

then
later
behind
next
following
subsequently
afterwards
thereafter

15

agree
(disagree)

admit
approve
consent
allow
concur
accede
agreement
agreeable

16

alarm
(soothe)

startle
shock

arouse
warn
scare
frighten
[see 216, 239, 587, 710]

17

alike
(different)

like
similar
resembling
related
equal
matching
likeness

18

alive
(dead)

living
lively
vigorous
active
energetic
robust
[see 813]

19

all
(none)

everyone
everybody
everything
the whole
the sum
the total

20

allow
(forbid)

let
permit
grant
admit
endure
authorise
allowable
allowance
[see 346, 473]

21

almost

about
nearly
barely
scarcely
approaching
virtually
[see 421]

22

alone
(together)

lonely
separated
deserted
apart
abandoned
solitary
[see 445, 630]

23

always
(never)

ever
evermore
forever
endlessly
constantly
perpetually
[see 203]

24

among
(around)

between
amidst

contd.

amongst
amid
surrounded by
encompassed by

25

amuse
(bore)

please
entertain
cheer
gladden
charm
interest
amusing
amusement

26

angry
(calm)

cross
annoyed
displeased
furious
upset
enraged
anger
[see 153, 728]

27

animal

creature
mammal
bird
fish
reptile
insect

28

another

extra
second
additional
further
separate
supplementary

29

answer
(question)

reply
response
retort
rejoinder
explanation
solution
answerable
[see 548]

30

appear
(disappear)

arrive
attend
arise
dawn
loom
emerge
appearance

31

area

field
district
region
zone
locality
territory
[see 147, 179, 840]

32

argue
(agree)

disagree
debate
discuss
dispute
reason
plead
argument

33

army

soldiers
troops
forces
legion
host
multitude

34

around
(amid)

about
surrounding
enfolding
encircling
enveloping
encompassing

35

ask
(answer)

request
beg
demand
enquire
invite
implore
[see 313]

36

asleep
(awake)

sleeping
slumbering
dozing
resting
reposing
unconscious
sleepy
slept

37

attack
(defend)

raid
rush
storm
charge
besiege
assault

38

attitude

manner
mood
behaviour
expression
bearing
demeanour
[see 378]

39

attractive
(repulsive)

pleasing
pretty
delightful
interesting
appealing
fascinating
attract
attraction
[see 222]

40

author

writer
compiler
poet
creator
composer
originator

41

average
(extreme)

usual
ordinary
normal
medium
moderate
commonplace

42

awake
(asleep)

alert
watchful
ready
attentive
conscious
vigilant
awakening
awoke
awoken
[see 797]

43

away
(near)

far
gone
absent
abroad
distant
remote

44

awful
(pleasant)

bad
nasty
dreadful
frightening
startling
alarming
awfully
[see 731, 732]

45

awkward
(dexterous)

clumsy
unskilful
ungainly
ungraceful
inexpert
maladroit
awkwardness

46

baby
(adult)

babe
infant
toddler
child
newborn
innocent
babies
babyish

47

bad
(good)

evil
wicked
mean
faulty
harmful
unpleasant
badly
[see 416, 818]

48

bag

sack
satchel
case
grip
pouch
rucksack
baggage
bagged

49

ball

globe
sphere
orb
pellet
globule
projectile

50
band

group
team
gang
company
gathering
orchestra
[see 122, 133, 604, 725, 781]

51
bang

knock
beat
crash
shot
report
explosion

52
bar

rod
pole
shaft
stake
barrier
obstacle
barred
[see 490, 566, 682]

53
bare
(covered)

uncovered
undressed
naked
nude
bald
exposed

54
battle
(peace)

fight
struggle
contest
warfare
combat
conflict
battlefield
[see 138, 220, 802]

55
beach

shore
seaside
sands
coast
shingle
strand
beached
[see 123, 616]

56
beat
(caress)

hit
thump
thrash
batter
knock
defeat
[see 167, 289, 314, 815]

57
beautiful
(ugly)

pretty
handsome
lovely
enchanting
superb
exquisite
beauty
beautify
[see 369, 504]

58

become

be
grow
develop
mature
convert
evolve
becoming
became
[see 263]

59

before
(after)

in front
ahead
earlier
sooner
previously
hitherto
beforehand

60

begin
(end)

start
commence
launch
originate
establish
initiate
beginning
begun
began
[see 672]

61

believe
(doubt)

think
guess
suppose
hope
trust
suspect
belief
[see 708, 771]

62

bench

seat
form
pew
settle
workbench
counter
[see 102, 594]

63

bend
(straighten)

curve
turn
twist
wind
swerve
flex
bent

64

beside

next to
near
at hand
abreast
alongside
adjacent to
[see 120, 420]

65

big
(little)

large
great
huge
enormous
massive
tremendous
bigger

biggest
[see 260, 261, 335]

66

bill

charge
fee
account
statement
invoice
reckoning

67

bite

nip
sting
snap
crunch
eat
chew
biting
bitten

68

blank

empty
bare
plain
vacant
barren
void
[see 196, 294, 787]

69

boat

ship
yacht
canoe
craft
vessel
dinghy
[see 613, 760]

70

body

creature
human
person
mortal
corpse
carcass
bodily
[see 376, 474]

71

book

volume
booklet
manual
paperback
brochure
tome
bookish
bookworm

72

boring
(exciting)

dull
tiring
wearying
tedious
unexciting
monotonous
bore
bored

73

boss
(worker)

chief
head
master
manager
director
executive
bossy
[see 92, 109]

74

bother
(peace)

trouble
worry
annoyance
vexation
irritation
inconvenience
bothersome
[see 435, 769]

75

box

container
crate
chest
cabinet
trunk
casket
boxed
[see 97]

76

boy
(girl)

lad
youngster
kid
urchin
youth
adolescent
boys
boyish

77

brave
(timid)

bold
fearless
daring
courageous
heroic
valiant
bravery
[see 148]

78

break
(mend)

smash
shatter
split
fracture
sever
destroy
broken
broke
[see 150, 645]

79

bright
(dull)

shining
dazzling
brilliant
radiant
glittering
scintillating
brightness
brightly

80

bring
(take)

get
fetch
gather
deliver
escort
invite
brought
[see 218]

81

broken
(mended)

damaged
smashed
shattered
fractured

destroyed
ruptured

82

build
(destroy)

make
construct
assemble
erect
devise
establish
built

83

bump

shock
jolt
hit
thump
knock
collide

84

burn
(extinguish)

flicker
blaze
glow
glare
ignite
incinerate
burnt

85

bury
(expose)

hide
cover
conceal
secrete
entomb
inter
burying
buried
[see 149, 285]

86

bus

omnibus
coach
motorcoach
railbus
pullman
vehicle
buses

87

business
(pleasure)

job
work
trade
employment
career
occupation
businesslike

88

busy
(lazy)

working
active
lively
occupied
engaged
industrious

89

buy
(sell)

get
obtain
purchase
hire
procure
acquire
buying

contd.

bought
[see 438]

90

call
(listen)

cry
shout
yell
exclaim
scream
bellow
[see 156, 591]

91

calm
(disturbed)

quiet
peaceful
undisturbed
restful
tranquil
placid
calmness
[see 467, 529, 626]

92

captain

leader
headman
chief
commander
officer
skipper
[see 73, 109]

93

capture
(release)

take
catch
seize
arrest
imprison
apprehend
capturing
[see 99]

94

car

motorcar
saloon
vehicle
automobile
taxi
limousine
[see 760, 790]

95

careful
(careless)

watchful
attentive
thoughtful
cautious
wary
conscientious
care
carefully

96

carry
(drop)

hold
lift
shift
bear
convey
transport
carrying
carried

97

case

box
carton
chest
crate

container
receptacle
[see 75]

98

castle

fort
tower
keep
stronghold
fortress
citadel
[see 754]

99

catch
(miss)

take
grasp
snatch
grip
seize
clutch
caught
[see 93]

100

cave

cavern
den
grotto
hollow
dugout
cavity
cavernous

101

certain
(doubtful)

sure
satisfied
positive
undoubted
undeniable
convinced
certainty
certainly
[see 709]

102

chair

seat
armchair
easychair
rocking chair
wing chair
throne
chairman
chairwoman
[see 62, 594]

103

change
(conserve)

alter
transform
convert
reconstruct
modify
reorganise
changeable
changeless

104

chase

follow
pursue
hunt
trail
track
shadow
chasing
[see 230, 303, 758]

105

cheap
(dear)

inexpensive
common
poor
mean
shabby

contd.

worthless
cheapness

106

cheat

trick
swindle
defraud
hoodwink
deceive
exploit
[see 767]

107

cheer

shout
hurrah
applaud
praise
encourage
reassure
[see 562, 618]

108

cheerful
(dejected)

glad
happy
joyful
merry
jolly
lively
cheerfulness
cheerfully
[see 248, 255, 270]

109

chief
(follower)

leader
head
ruler
chieftain
lord
commander
[see 73, 92]

110

child
(adult)

youngster
son/daughter
infant
offspring
progeny
descendant
children
[see 839]

111

choke

gag
retch
stifle
strangle
suffocate
asphyxiate

112

choose
(reject)

pick
select
separate
judge
prefer
favour
choice
[see 475, 654]

113

citizen

dweller
inhabitant
resident
subject
civilian
householder
[see 755]

114

clean (adj)
(dirty)

washed
unsoiled
spotless
unstained
fresh
pure
cleanliness

115

clean (v)
(pollute)

wash
cleanse
polish
wipe
scrub
scour
[see 711, 804]

116

clear

light
bright
clean
visible
lucid
transparent
clearly
clarity

117

clever
(stupid)

sharp
bright
gifted
smart
intelligent
precocious
cleverness

118

climb
(descend)

clamber
scramble
mount
scale
ascend
surmount
[see 558]

119

close
(open)

shut
bolt
lock
fasten
block
obstruct
closing
closure
[see 359, 620]

120

close
(distant)

near
nearby
next to
neighbouring
adjoining
bordering
closeness
closely
[see 64, 420, 426]

121

clothing

clothes
garments
dress
uniform
costume
attire
clothed
[see 145, 184]

122
club

group
team
gang
company
society
association
[see 50, 133, 604, 725]

123
coast

coastline
shore
foreshore
strand
shoreline
seaboard
coastal
[see 55, 616]

124
coat

jacket
blazer
sportscoat
overcoat
raincoat
greatcoat

125
code

morse
braille
standard
guideline
cipher
cryptogram

126
cold
(hot)

cool
chilly
frosty
icy
wintry
arctic
coldness
coldly

127
collect
(scatter)

gather
save
hoard
pile
reserve
accumulate
collection
[see 247]

128
colour

hue
tint
shade
tone
tinge
complexion

129
come
(go)

arrive
appear
reach
approach
enter
advance
coming
came

130
comfortable
(uncomfortable)

warm
cosy

snug
contented
peaceful
relaxed
comfort
comfortably
[see 803]

131

comic
(sad)

funny
amusing
witty
laughable
humorous
ludicrous
comical

132

common
(rare)

ordinary
plain
simple
everyday
usual
familiar
commonplace
[see 105, 786]

133

company
(individual)

group
gathering
assembly
society
association
meeting
companies
[see 50, 122, 154, 725]

134

compare

liken
balance
measure
contrast
collate
differentiate
comparing
comparison

135

complete
(incomplete)

whole
total
entire
finished
achieved
perfect
completing
completion
[see 470]

136

confuse
(clarify)

puzzle
baffle
bewilder
mystify
disconcert
perplex
confusing
confusion
[see 525]

137

contain

hold
carry
enclose
include
accommodate
incorporate

138

contest
(agreement)

fight
struggle
dispute
match
competition
conflict
[see 54, 220, 527, 802]

139

continual

nonstop
endless
ceaseless
constant
incessant
interminable
continually

140

continuous

continued
connected
unbroken
entire
consecutive
progressive
continuation

141

control

rule
govern
direct
manage
supervise
dominate
controlling
controlled
[see 575]

142

copy
(originate)

rewrite
imitate
duplicate
trace
forge
reproduce
copies
copied

143

correct
(incorrect)

right
exact
true
proper
accurate
faultless
correction
[see 515, 555, 770]

144

cost

price
payment
charge
value
expense
expenditure
costly
[see 506]

145

costume

dress
clothing
garments
robe
uniform
attire
[see 121, 184]

146

count

number
tally
score
total
reckon
calculate

147

country

kingdom
nation
realm
district
region
territory
[see 31, 179, 840]

148

courage

bravery
boldness
gallantry
fortitude
heroism
valour
courageous
[see 77]

149

cover
(expose)

wrap
hide
conceal
protect
shelter
secrete
[see 85, 285, 568, 835]

150

crack

break
opening
gap
cleft
fracture
fissure
[see 78, 292, 645]

151

crash

smash
wreck
bump
bang
explode
collide
[see 3]

152

crime

wrong
fault
sin
misdeed
offence
felony
criminal

153

cross
(pleased)

angry
upset
annoyed
bothered
vexed
irritated
[see 26, 728]

154

crowd
(individual)

group
gathering
assembly
crush
mass
mob
[see 133, 436]

155

cruel
(kind)

unkind
beastly
brutal
heartless
pitiless
diabolical
cruelty
[see 219, 583]

156

cry
(laugh)

scream
shout
yell
sob
weep
blubber
crying
cried
[see 90, 591]

157

cut

divide
slice
chop
slit
carve
sever
cutting
cutter
[see 181]

158

damage
(repair)

harm
injury
accident
mischief
destruction
vandalism
damaging
[see 664]

159

damp
(dry)

wet
moist
clammy
soggy
steamy
humid
dampness
[see 814]

160

danger
(safety)

risk
hazard
threat
peril
menace
jeopardy
dangerous

161

dark
(light)

black
dim
shady
unlit
murky
ebony
darkness
[see 606]

162

dated
(new)

out of date
old fashioned
outmoded
antiquated
obsolete

obsolescent
[see 444, 463]

163

dawn
(sunset)

sunrise
daybreak
daylight
sun-up
cock-crow
morning

164

dead
(alive)

lifeless
gone
departed
deceased
defunct
extinct
death

165

dear
(cheap)

costly
high-priced
expensive
excessive
extortionate
exorbitant
[see 206]

166

decide
(waive)

settle
consider
determine
conclude
evaluate
arbitrate
deciding
decision
[see 223]

167

defeat
(surrender)

beat
conquer
overcome
rout
vanquish
subjugate
[see 56]

168

delay
(hasten)

stop
hinder
check
defer
postpone
procrastinate
[see 688]

169

delicious
(disgusting)

tasty
dainty
appetising
toothsome
luscious
delectable
delicacy
[see 712, 722]

170

delighted
(disappointed)

pleased
happy
overjoyed
thrilled
jubilant

contd.

ecstatic
delight
delightful
[see 108, 270]

171

desert
(stay)

leave
quit
abandon
forsake
defect
betray
[see 344]

172

destroy
(create)

wreck
shatter
ruin
demolish
ravage
devastate
destruction

173

dig

scoop
plough
cultivate
unearth
delve
excavate
digging
dug

174

dip

duck
plunge
sink
soak
bathe
immerse
dipping
dipped

175

dirty
(clean)

unclean
filthy
unwashed
foul
grimy
squalid
dirtiness

176

discover

find
detect
notice
recognise
locate
unearth
discovery
[see 221]

177

disease
(health)

illness
sickness
ailment
ill-health
infection
disability
diseased
[see 308, 622]

178

dish

plate
saucer
bowl
tureen

crock
salver

179

district

area
region
zone
parish
locality
territory
[see 31, 147, 840]

180

ditch

drain
trench
channel
moat
dyke
culvert

181

divide
(join)

share
separate
sever
split
disconnect
detach
division
[see 157, 601, 663]

182

do
(neglect)

carry out
perform
make
finish
complete
accomplish
did
done
[see 375]

183

dodge

shift
duck
swerve
shuffle
evade
recoil
dodging

184

dress

frock
gown
robe
costume
suit
outfit
[see 121, 145]

185

drink (v)

swallow
sup
sip
gulp
imbibe
absorb
drank
drunk

186

drink (n)

liquid
beverage
nightcap
refreshment
cup of
draught

187

drop

fall
sink
lower
droop
drip
descend
dropping
dropped
[see 209]

188

dry
(wet)

thirsty
parched
rainless
waterless
stale
dehydrated
dried
[see 741]

189

dull

dim
cloudy
dismal
dreary
boring
cheerless

190

early
(late)

beforehand
timely
previous
prompt
immediate
premature
[see 651]

191

earth

soil
land
ground
turf
dirt
clay
[see 262, 333, 647]

192

easily

handily
simply
smoothly
skilfully
effortlessly
adroitly

193

easy
(difficult)

simple
plain
obvious
effortless
uncomplicated
facile
easily
[see 628]

194

eat
(starve)

feed
chew
munch
gobble
devour
masticate
ate
eaten
[see 231]

195

edge
(centre)

border
rim
margin
verge
perimeter
periphery
edging
[see 623]

196

empty
(full)

unfilled
vacant
unoccupied
void
drained
uninhabited
emptied
[see 68, 294, 787]

197

end
(beginning)

finish
ending
close
completion
conclusion
termination
[see 223, 336]

198

enemy
(friend)

foe
rival
opponent
attacker
adversary
antagonist
enemies

199

energy
(lethargy)

power
vigour
stamina
enterprise
vitality
initiative
energetic
[see 393, 695]

200

enjoy
(detest)

like
love
fancy
appreciate
savour
relish
enjoyable
[see 320, 354]

201

enough
(insufficient)

plenty
ample
sufficient
plentiful
abundant
adequate
[see 365, 379, 488]

202

even
(variable)

level
flat

contd.

smooth
straight
equal
balanced
evenness
[see 226, 347, 644, 692]

203

ever
(never)

always
forever
evermore
continually
repeatedly
perpetually
[see 23]

204

exchange

change
swap
barter
trade
substitute
reciprocate
exchanging
[see 757]

205

exciting
(dull)

thrilling
stirring
startling
arousing
hair-raising
stimulating
excite
excitable

206

expensive
(cheap)

dear
costly
unreasonable
excessive
exorbitant
extortionate
expense
[see 165]

207

fact
(fiction)

truth
information
reality
data
certainty
actuality
factual
[see 772]

208

fade
(last)

disappear
vanish
wither
blanch
pale
decline
fading

209

fall
(rise)

drop
sink
descend
slip
trip
plummet
fallen
fell
[see 187, 637, 768]

210

famous
(unknown)

well-known
famed
honoured
remarkable
celebrated
distinguished
fame

211

far
(near)

distant
far-off
removed
long
remote
inaccessible

212

farm

grange
farmstead
smallholding
croft
ranch
manor

213

fast
(slow)

quick
rapid
speedy
swift
express
accelerated
[see 528, 714]

214

fasten
(detach)

tie
bind
join
attach
fix
secure
[see 225, 318, 745]

215

fat
(thin)

plump
tubby
portly
overweight
corpulent
obese
[see 737]

216

fear
(courage)

fright
alarm
dread
terror
dismay
horror
fearful
[see 16, 239]

217

feast
(famine)

meal
banquet
barbecue
festival
anniversary
celebration
[see 231, 384]

218

fetch

get
bring

contd.

carry
convey
escort
transport
[see 80]

219

fierce
(tame)

wild
savage
furious
violent
vicious
cruel
[see 155, 583, 820]

220

fight
(peace)

combat
contest
battle
conflict
brawl
quarrel
fought
[see 54, 138, 527, 699, 802]

221

find
(lose)

discover
detect
observe
notice
recognise
locate
found
[see 176]

222

fine
(displeasing)

good
satisfactory
splendid
excellent
pleasing
admirable
[see 39, 258]

223

finish
(begin)

end
complete
settle
terminate
conclude
accomplish
[see 166, 197, 688]

224

fire

flame
blaze
bonfire
spark
ignition
combustion

225

fix
(damage)

fasten
join
connect
mend
repair
arrange
[see 214, 318, 745]

226

flat
(uneven)

level
even
smooth
plane

horizontal
prostrate
flatter
[see 202, 347, 644]

227

flow

move
run
pour
stream
glide
undulate

228

fly

hover
glide
soar
zoom
dart
aviate
flight
flew
flown

229

folk

people
persons
public
family
relatives
nation
folklore
[see 469, 494]

230

follow
(lead)

go after
go behind
chase
hunt
pursue
shadow
[see 104, 303, 758]

231

food

foodstuffs
meal
fare
diet
menu
nourishment
[see 194, 217, 384]

232

forget
(remember)

overlook
omit
neglect
ignore
disregard
leave behind
forgot
forgotten
forgetful

233

fortune
(poverty)

money
wealth
riches
luck
chance
fate
fortunate
fortunately
[see 404, 763]

234

forward
(backward)

onward
ahead

contd.

toward
advance
progress
move on

235

frank
(evasive)

honest
open
sincere
candid
forthright
ingenuous
[see 296]

236

free
(slave)

let out
released
at liberty
loose
unchained
unbound
freedom
[see 348, 446]

237

fresh
(stale)

new
latest
modern
recent
new-grown
lively
freshness
[see 402, 425]

238

friend
(enemy)

pal
mate
chum
comrade
companion
confidant
friendship
[see 460]

239

fright
(calm)

fear
scare
alarm
terror
dread
horror
frightful
frightfully
[see 13, 16, 216]

240

full
(empty)

filled
brimming
crammed
packed
stuffed
crowded
[see 241]

241

fully
(partly)

totally
entirely
plentifully
generously
thoroughly
completely
[see 240]

242

fun
(sadness)

pleasure
enjoyment
amusement
laughter
gladness
celebration
[see 487]

243

funny
(sad)

amusing
comical
witty
laughable
humorous
hilarious
funnily

244

gain
(lose)

get
win
gather
collect
obtain
increase
[see 251, 438, 717]

245

game
(work)

play
pastime
amusement
sport
competition
recreation
gamesmanship
[see 486, 665]

246

gang

band
group
crew
set
pack
troop
[see 50, 154]

247

gather
(scatter)

pick
collect
pile up
reap
harvest
assemble
[see 127]

248

gay
(sad)

merry
happy
cheerful
joyful
lively
vivacious
gaiety
[see 108, 255, 270]

249

gentle
(rough)

tender
kind
mild
soothing
humane
considerate
gentleness
gently
[see 328, 720, 729]

250

germ

bug
microbe
bacteria
virus
bacillus
micro-organism

251

get
(lose)

earn
receive
obtain
bring
fetch
acquire
getting
got
[see 2, 244, 438, 536, 539, 717]

252

gift
(forfeit)

present
favour
grant
offering
donation
bequest
[see 502]

253

girl
(boy)

lass
maiden
damsel
female
woman
young lady

254

give
(take)

offer
afford
supply
spare
donate
contribute
gave

255

glad
(sorry)

happy
pleased
delighted
thrilled
contented
satisfied
gladness
gladly
[see 108, 248, 270]

256

glass

beaker
crystal
tumbler
wineglass
goblet
chalice

257

go
(come)

move
walk
travel
set out
leave
depart
going
gone
went
[see 409]

258

good
(bad)

right
true
pure
honest
satisfactory
excellent
goodness
[see 222, 470]

259

grab

snatch
seize
catch
grip
clutch
takeover
grabbed
[see 291]

260

grand
(modest)

large
great
splendid
noble
majestic
magnificent
grandeur
[see 65, 335, 662]

261

great
(small)

big
large
huge
vast
immense
gigantic
greatness
[see 65, 260, 335]

262

ground

soil
earth
land
turf
field
terrain
[see 191, 333, 647]

263

grow
(decline)

increase
enlarge
expand
develop
extend
thrive
grew
grown
[see 58, 311]

264

guard
(neglect)

watch
protect
defend
shelter
shield
preserve
[see 517, 584]

265

guess

think
believe
imagine
judge
suppose

contd.

suspect
[see 708, 740, 827]

266

guide
(mislead)

lead
steer
direct
drive
accompany
navigate
guidance
[see 342, 679]

267

gun

pistol
revolver
automatic
shotgun
rifle
cannon

268

hair

curl
ringlet
tress
lock
fringe
plait

269

hang
(stand)

swing
cling
dangle
hitch
suspend
append
hung
[see 715]

270

happy
(unhappy)

pleased
contented
satisfied
untroubled
carefree
gratified
happiness
happily
[see 108, 170, 248, 255]

271

harbour

port
anchorage
shelter
refuge
haven
sanctuary
[see 611]

272

hard
(soft)

firm
solid
rigid
resistant
compact
rocky
hardness
[see 648, 683, 753]

273

harm
(benefit)

hurt
injure
damage
wound
spoil
ruin

harmful
[see 305, 834]

274

hat

cap
beret
helmet
turban
bowler
hood

275

hate
(love)

dislike
detest
loathe
despise
abominate
abhor
hatred

276

have
(need)

own
possess
hold
keep
use
retain
had
having
[see 291]

277

head

skull
brain
mind
intelligence
wisdom
genius
[see 395]

278

heal
(wound)

soothe
mend
cure
repair
restore
renew
health
[see 437]

279

healthy
(unhealthy)

fit
well
strong
hearty
robust
vigorous
[see 698, 813]

280

heap

pile
mound
collection
mass
hoard
accumulation
[see 479]

281

hear
(ignore)

listen
attend
heed
learn
understand
comprehend

contd.

hearing
heard

282

heat
(cold)

warmth
hotness
temperature
fever
flush
fire
hot
hotter
[see 300, 803]

283

heavy
(light)

weighty
hefty
massive
bulky
cumbersome
ponderous
heaviness
heavily
[see 358]

284

help
(hinder)

aid
assist
support
serve
encourage
oblige
[see 603, 707]

285

hide
(reveal)

cover
conceal
screen
disguise
secrete
camouflage
hid
hidden
[see 85, 149, 835]

286

high
(low)

tall
lofty
steep
towering
soaring
elevated
height
heighten
[see 361, 719]

287

hike

walk
ramble
tramp
wander
march
roam
hiking
[see 381, 759, 798]

288

hill
(valley)

hillock
mount
highland
moor
slope
incline

289

hit
(stroke)

beat
knock
strike
hurt
smack
collide
hitting
[see 56, 314, 815]

290

hobby
(job)

pastime
amusement
recreation
pursuit
sideline
relaxation
hobbies

291

hold
(drop)

grip
grasp
clutch
clasp
keep
retain
held
[see 259, 276, 326, 752]

292

hole

opening
gap
aperture
hollow
pit
cavity
[see 150]

293

holiday
(workday)

day off
festival
celebration
carnival
anniversary
leave

294

hollow
(solid)

empty
not solid
unfilled
drained
indented
excavated
[see 68, 196]

295

home

house
residence
dwelling
abode
lodging
habitation
[see 301]

296

honest
(dishonest)

fair
true
just
trusty
sincere
incorruptible
honesty
[see 235, 297]

297

honour
(dishonour)

fairness
justice
honesty
sincerity
trust
conscience
honourable
[see 296]

298

hope
(despair)

wanting
wishing
longing
desire
faith
expectation
hopeful

299

horse

pony
mare
stallion
steed
mount
thoroughbred

300

hot
(cold)

heated
burning
boiling
fiery
flaming
scalding
heat
[see 282, 803]

301

house

cottage
bungalow
manor
mansion
grange
palace
housing
[see 295]

302

hungry
(satisfied)

peckish
famished
starving
greedy
ravenous
voracious
hunger

303

hunt

look for
seek
search
chase
track
pursue
[see 104, 230, 593, 758]

304

hurry
(dawdle)

quicken
move
hasten
rush
accelerate
expedite
hurried

305

hurt
(heal)

harm
bruise

wound
torture
mutilate
maim
[see 273, 834]

306

idea

thought
opinion
belief
plan
scheme
suspicion
[see 742]

307

ignore
(notice)

pass
skip
disregard
overlook
neglect
omit
ignorance

308

ill
(well)

unwell
sick
ailing
unhealthy
diseased
indisposed
illness
[see 177, 622]

309

important
(trivial)

serious
urgent
notable
worthy
significant
momentous
importance
[see 602]

310

improve
(spoil)

mend
correct
rectify
refurbish
enhance
perfect
improvement

311

increase
(decrease)

enlarge
extend
expand
stretch
inflate
magnify
increasing
[see 263]

312

information
(ignorance)

knowledge
facts
advice
instruction
wisdom
intelligence
inform
informant
[see 11]

313

invite
(forbid)

ask
request
beckon
appeal
entice
summon
invitation
[see 35]

314

jab

poke
prod
dig
nudge
punch
inject
jabbing
jabbed
[see 56, 289]

315

jail
(freedom)

prison
gaol
lockup
guardhouse
detention centre
penitentiary
[see 509]

316

jealous
(content)

envious
suspicious
distrustful
covetous
resentful
begrudging
jealousy

317

job
(hobby)

work
task
business
employment
occupation
profession
jobbing
[see 331, 440, 497, 831]

318

join
(part)

connect
fasten
couple
link
combine
unite
[see 214, 225, 745, 782]

319

journey

trip
tour
voyage
outing
route
excursion
journeys
[see 762, 794]

320

joy
(sorrow)

happiness
gladness
pleasure
delight
excitement

ecstasy
joyful
[see 200]

321

judge

think
decide
determine
reckon
consider
conclude
judgement
[see 541, 777]

322

jump
(stand)

leap
spring
bound
vault
skip
pounce
[see 634, 669]

323

junk
(valuables)

rubbish
scrap
leavings
remnants
lumber
rejects

324

just

exactly
almost
simply
barely
hardly
recently
only just

325

keen
(indifferent)

eager
earnest
fiery
vigorous
intent
enthusiastic
keenness

326

keep
(reject)

hold
store
retain
possess
protect
preserve
kept
[see 291]

327

kill
(protect)

slay
murder
slaughter
assassinate
execute
annihilate
[see 412]

328

kind
(cruel)

good
tender
gentle
thoughtful
generous
considerate
kindness
kindly
[see 249, 729]

329

knock

rap
beat
hit
strike
punch
collide with

330

know
(misunderstand)

understand
realise
comprehend
recognise
perceive
discern
knew
knowledge
[see 343, 778]

331

labour
(rest)

work
job
employment
occupation
livelihood
toil
labourer
[see 317, 440, 831]

332

lady
(gentleman)

woman
female
girl
wife
mother
daughter
ladies

333

land

earth
ground
field
country
nation
kingdom
[see 191, 262, 417]

334

language

words
speech
talk
conversation
dialect
vocabulary
[see 830]

335

large
(small)

big
huge
massive
enormous
immense
gigantic
[see 65, 260, 261]

336

last
(first)

latest
final
rearmost
end
utmost
concluding
[see 197, 223]

337

late
(early)

delayed
slow

behind
overdue
unpunctual
belated
lateness
[see 638]

338

laugh
(cry)

chuckle
giggle
snigger
titter
cackle
guffaw
laughter
[see 642]

339

law
(misrule)

rule
control
command
regulation
order
directive
lawful

340

lay
(remove)

put
place
set
rest
deposit
arrange
laid
[see 524]

341

lazy
(industrious)

idle
listless
shiftless
slack
inactive
indolent
laziness

342

lead
(follow)

go before
guide
escort
direct
conduct
precede
led
[see 266, 679]

343

learn

find out
discover
understand
memorise
comprehend
perceive
[see 330, 700, 778]

344

leave
(arrive)

go away
depart
abandon
desert
withdraw
vacate
left
[see 171]

345

length
(width)

measure
reach
span
distance
dimension
magnitude
long
lengthy

346

let
(forbid)

allow
permit
consent
enable
tolerate
acquiesce
letting
[see 20, 473]

347

level

even
flat
smooth
flush
equal
balanced
levelled
[see 202, 226, 644]

348

liberty
(slavery)

freedom
choice
permission
release
discretion
privilege
[see 236]

349

lie

rest
recline
repose
relax
remain
continue
lay
[see 551]

350

life
(death)

being alive
existence
energy
vigour
nature
mankind
lively
[see 661]

351

lift
(drop)

raise
pull up
hoist
uplift
elevate
exhibit
[see 533]

352

light (1)
(dark)

brightness
shine
glow
glare
gleam

illumination
lit
[see 612]

353

light (2)
(heavy)

unweighty
weightless
buoyant
portable
delicate
flimsy
lightness

354

like
(dislike)

enjoy
love
fancy
adore
relish
approve
[see 200, 368]

355

line

mark
stroke
stripe
row
string
groove
[see 382]

356

little
(big)

small
tiny
undersized
miniature
diminutive
microscopic
[see 639, 748]

357

live
(die)

be alive
exist
thrive
endure
survive
flourish
life
living

358

load

weight
burden
freight
cargo
pack
encumbrance
[see 283]

359

lock
(unlock)

close
fasten
clasp
seal
bolt
secure
[see 119, 620]

360

lone
(accompanied)

lonely
alone
single
apart
solitary
isolated
loneliness

361

long
(short)

lengthy
extended
tall
outstretched
elongated
protracted
length
[see 286, 719]

362

look
(disregard)

see
watch
gaze
stare
observe
contemplate
[see 433, 596, 806]

363

loose
(tight)

undone
slack
untied
free
unfastened
sagging
[see 545, 779]

364

lose
(find)

mislay
drop
miss
fail
forget
forfeit
losing
lost
[see 399]

365

lots
(little)

much
quantity
load
mass
many
numerous
[see 201, 379, 488]

366

loud
(soft)

noisy
deafening
clamorous
uproarious
sonorous
thundering
[see 428, 572, 744]

367

love (n)
(hatred)

friendship
affection
fondness
devotion
ardour
adoration
loving
[see 368]

368

love (v)
(hate)

like
admire

cherish
esteem
treasure
adore
loving
[see 354, 367]

369

lovely
(hideous)

pleasing
attractive
beautiful
delightful
enchanting
captivating
loveliness
[see 57, 487, 504]

370

low
(high)

under
sunk
deep
depressed
buried
submerged

371

luck
(purpose)

chance
fortune
fate
hazard
success
destiny

372

machine

motor
engine
tool
gadget
apparatus
appliance
[see 750]

373

mad
(sane)

crazy
insane
lunatic
demented
deranged
unbalanced
madness

374

main
(minor)

first
leading
foremost
important
principal
cardinal
[see 507]

375

make
(destroy)

create
construct
produce
shape
devise
manufacture
making
made
[see 182]

376

man
(woman)

gentleman
male

contd.

boy
husband
father
son
men
[see 70, 474]

377

manage
(mismanage)

run
direct
control
regulate
supervise
administer
management

378

manner

conduct
behaviour
style
habit
custom
demeanour
[see 38]

379

many
(few)

lots
plenty
numerous
abundant
countless
copious
[see 201, 365, 383, 436, 488, 789]

380

map

diagram
plan
chart
plot
representation
projection
mapping

381

march

stride
parade
swagger
strut
advance
progress
[see 287, 759, 798]

382

mark

stamp
label
brand
sign
distinguish
differentiate
[see 355, 666]

383

mass
(fragment)

store
supply
stock
collection
accumulation
profusion
[see 379]

384

meal

feed
feast
repast
banquet
barbecue
collation
[see 217, 231]

385

measure

rule
divide
gauge
estimate
apportion
partition
measuring
measured
[see 526, 632]

386

meet
(avoid)

find
see
greet
welcome
encounter
confront
met
[see 221, 812]

387

melt
(solidify)

soften
thaw
fuse
dissolve
liquefy
liquidise

388

merry
(miserable)

happy
cheerful
gay
joyful
amiable
convivial
merriment

389

mess
(order)

muddle
jumble
clutter
filth
disorder
confusion

390

message

news
note
information
despatch
missive
communication
messenger

391

method
(muddle)

way
plan
system
scheme
design
technique
[see 448, 484, 716, 808]

392

middle
(edge)

centre
midpoint
midst
medium
equidistant
median
middling

393

might
(weakness)

strength
power
force
vigour
prowess
invincibility
mightily
[see 199, 394, 498, 695, 698]

394

mighty
(weak)

powerful
unbeatable
irresistible
dynamic
invincible
overwhelming
mightiness
[see 393]

395

mind
(body)

brain
sense
reason
mentality
intelligence
intellect
[see 277]

396

mine

pit
quarry
colliery
excavation
seam
lode
mining

397

miss

drop
lose
bungle
slip up
disregard
miscalculate

398

missile

spear
shot
bomb
rocket
torpedo
projectile

399

missing
(found)

lost
gone
absent
astray
mislaid
misplaced
[see 364]

400

mistake

fault
error
flaw
blunder
inaccuracy
miscalculation
mistook

401

mix
(separate)

mingle
jumble
blend

combine
unite
amalgamate
mixture

402

modern
(ancient)

new
fresh
up-to-date
recent
fashionable
current
[see 237,425]

403

moment

instant
second
minute
flash
point
juncture
momentarily
[see 747]

404

money

cash
coins
notes
change
wealth
affluence
[see 233, 763]

405

more
(less)

greater
extra
gain
further
increase
additional
most
[see 449]

406

motion
(rest)

moving
movement
action
travel
progress
mobility
motor
[see 257, 409]

407

motive

reason
cause
purpose
design
stimulus
incentive
motivate
motivation
[see 522]

408

mountain
(ravine)

highland
peak
crest
ridge
summit
pinnacle
mountainous
[see 468]

409

move

go
depart

contd.

set forth
stir
advance
progress
moving
movable
[see 257, 406]

410

mud

dirt
muck
clay
silt
sludge
morass
muddy
muddied
[see 411]

411

muddy
(clear)

mucky
slushy
boggy
marshy
swampy
turbid
[see 410]

412

murder

kill
slay
slaughter
massacre
exterminate
assassinate
murdered
[see 327]

413

music

sound
tone
melody
harmony
rhythm
composition
musician
[see 650, 655, 774]

414

name

title
surname
forename
designation
classification
appelation
nominal

415

narrow
(wide)

thin
slender
cramped
limited
confined
attenuated
narrowness
[see 739]

416

nasty
(nice)

bad
ugly
foul
loathsome
repulsive
abhorrent
nastiness
nastily
[see 47, 818]

417

nation

land
country

kingdom
realm
state
republic
national
[see 333]

418

natural
(unnatural)

real
pure
usual
normal
genuine
authentic
naturally
[see 521]

419

naughty

bad
wicked
mischievous
disobedient
undisciplined
perverse
naughtiness

420

near
(far)

by
close
next to
handy
adjoining
neighbouring
nearness
[see 64, 120, 426]

421

nearly

almost
closely
roughly
approaching
virtually
approximately
[see 21]

422

neat
(untidy)

smart
tidy
orderly
spruce
shipshape

unpretentious
[see 640]

423

need
(possess)

want
lack
require
demand
desire
crave
[see 492, 801, 826]

424

nervous
(bold)

shy
weak
timid
scared
fearful
hesitant
nervousness
[see 621]

425

new
(old)

fresh
unused

contd.

recent
novel
latest
modern
newness
[see 237, 402]

426

next
(previous)

after
later
closest
nearest
following
ensuing
[see 120, 420]

427

nice
(nasty)

pleasant
enjoyable
delightful
agreeable
attractive
exquisite
nicely
[see 369]

428

noise
(silence)

sound
row
din
uproar
clamour
commotion
noisy
noisily
[see 366, 572, 655, 744]

429

none
(some)

nil
nothing
nought
zero
non-existence
nullity
not one
[see 432]

430

nonsense
(sense)

folly
silliness
foolishness
stupidity
absurdity
inanity
nonsensical

431

note

letter
report
comment
record
draft
synopsis

432

nothing

none
nought
nil
zero
nullity
insignificance
[see 429]

433

notice
(miss)

see
discover

recognise
observe
perceive
discern
noticing
noticeable
[see 362, 543, 596, 806]

434

now
(then)

at present
today
straight away
immediately
instantly
nowadays

435

nuisance
(pleasure)

trouble
bother
annoyance
irritant
inconvenience
tribulation
[see 74, 769]

436

number

group
crowd
mob
host
throng
multitude
[see 154, 379]

437

nurse
(neglect)

care
attend
treat
tend
nourish
cherish
nursing
[see 278]

438

obtain
(lose)

get
gain
win
gather
procure
acquire
[see 89, 244, 251, 717]

439

obvious
(obscure)

plain
clear
visible
distinct
evident
apparent
obviousness
[see 116]

440

occupation

work
trade
craft
employment
business
profession
occupy
occupied
[see 317, 331, 442, 831]

441

odd
(ordinary)

strange
unusual
queer
quaint
uncommon
extraordinary
[see 693]

442

office

workplace
room
building
business
premises
headquarters
[see 317, 440]

443

often
(sometimes)

regularly
usually
frequently
repeatedly
periodically
habitually
[see 747]

444

old
(young)

elderly
aged
ancient
venerable
decrepit
senile
[see 162, 463]

445

only

single
alone
solitary
sole
exclusive
unique
[see 22, 630]

446

open
(closed)

clear
free
unlocked
unfastened
unobstructed
accessible
[see 236]

447

opinion
(fact)

idea
belief
view
feeling
judgement
appraisal
opinionated

448

order
(confusion)

plan
method
system
arrangement
organisation
harmony
orderly
orderliness
[see 391, 484, 716]

449

other
(same)

second
spare

extra
further
additional
supplementary
[see 405]

450

pack
(unpack)

fill
cram
load
store
compress
compact
[see 455]

451

pain
(pleasure)

hurt
ache
soreness
twinge
agony
torment
painful
[see 652, 685]

452

pale
(dark)

white
colourless
light
sallow
ashen
pallid
paleness
[see 817]

453

paper

sheet
newspaper
magazine
periodical
journal
publication

454

parade

show
display
procession
demonstration
spectacle
cavalcade
parading
[see 619]

455

parcel

bundle
packet
package
batch
bale
crate
parcelled
[see 450]

456

pardon
(punish)

forgive
excuse
clear
overlook
exonerate
reprieve

457

park

grassland
field
meadow
common
preserve
enclosure

458

part
(whole)

piece
share
portion
division
fragment
component
partly
partition
[see 478, 609]

459

particular
(general)

special
notable
unusual
remarkable
distinctive
exceptional
[see 659]

460

partner
(rival)

helper
companion
ally
accomplice
associate
colleague
partnership
[see 238]

461

pass

go by
move
proceed
overtake
advance
traverse
[see 257, 409]

462

passage

path
corridor
alley
entry
access
aisle
[see 464, 756]

463

past
(present)

ended
ago
former
bygone
prehistoric
archaic
[see 162, 444]

464

path
(obstruction)

way
footpath
track
trail
route
pavement
[see 462, 571, 756]

465

pause
(continue)

wait
delay
stay
hesitate
interrupt
discontinue
[see 546, 796]

466

pay
(owe)

give
reward
satisfy
settle
remunerate
reimburse
paid
[see 795]

467

peace
(disturbance)

rest
calm
quietness
silence
tranquillity
serenity
peaceful
[see 91, 529, 626]

468

peak
(base)

top
crest
summit
mountain
apex
eminence
[see 408, 489, 751]

469

people

human beings
individuals
folk
community
public
populace
[see 229, 494]

470

perfect
(faulty)

pure
faultless
ideal
exquisite
unblemished
immaculate
perfection
[see 135, 258, 828]

471

perhaps
(certainly)

maybe
possibly
probably
perchance
if possible
peradventure

472

period
(infinity)

time
season
term
spell
duration
era
periodic
[see 730, 747]

473

permission
(prohibition)

consent
agreement
approval
authority
assent

contd.

allowance
permit
permissive
[see 20, 346]

474

person

someone
somebody
human
individual
character
personality
[see 70, 376, 469]

475

pick
(reject)

choose
select
collect
gather
prefer
designate
[see 112, 654]

476

picnic

outing
treat
party
feast
barbecue
excursion
picnicking
[see 764]

477

picture

drawing
painting
sketch
photograph
portrait
illustration
picturesque

478

piece
(whole)

bit
part
scrap
portion
fragment
particle
[see 458, 609]

479

pile

heap
stack
mass
hump
collection
accumulation
[see 280, 686, 689]

480

pilot

guide
driver
leader
conductor
director
navigator
piloting
piloted
[see 266, 342, 679]

481

pirate

rover
buccaneer
raider
marauder
privateer

corsair
piracy
piratical

482

pitch
(retain)

fling
toss
hurl
heave
cast
propel
[see 743]

483

place

spot
position
site
district
neighbourhood
locality
[see 496, 674]

484

plan
(disorder)

idea
method
proposal
system
intent
scheme
planning
planned
[see 391, 448, 501, 522, 716, 808]

485

plant

flower
vegetable
shrub
bush
tree
herb

486

play
(work)

pastime
fun
game
sport
amusement
entertainment
[see 245, 665]

487

pleasant
(unpleasant)

pleasing
amusing
delightful
charming
gratifying
delectable
[see 242, 369]

488

plenty
(scarcity)

enough
sufficient
adequate
abundance
profusion
excess
plentiful
[see 201, 365, 379]

489

point

end
tip
spike
prong
peak

contd.

pinnacle
[see 468]

490

pole

stick
rod
post
mast
shaft
spar
[see 52, 566, 682]

491

polite

(rude)

graceful
civil
refined
gracious
mannerly
courteous
politeness
politely
[see 378]

492

poor

(rich)

needy
penniless
indigent
poverty-stricken
impoverished
destitute
poverty
[see 423, 531, 801]

493

popular

(unpopular)

liked
loved
admired
famous
approved
fashionable
popularity

494

population

people
citizens
folk
residents
inhabitants
populace
[see 229, 469]

495

port

seaport
harbour
dock
haven
anchorage
refuge

496

position

place
point
site
situation
location
emplacement
[see 483, 674]

497

post

job
work
living
employment
function
vocation
[see 317, 831]

498

power
(weakness)

strength
force
might
control
authority
domination
powerful
[see 393, 695, 698]

499

practice

habit
custom
procedure
routine
method
observance
[see 391]

500

practise

do
perform
prepare
exercise
rehearse
perpetrate
practising
[see 182]

501

prepare

make ready
arrange
plan
provide
equip
organise
preparation
preparatory
[see 484]

502

present

gift
prize
favour
donation
offering
contribution
presentation
[see 252]

503

press
(pull)

push
squeeze
crush
force
thrust
impel
pressure
[see 523]

504

pretty
(ugly)

pleasing
attractive
fair
lovely
dainty
captivating
prettiness
prettily
[see 57, 369]

505

prevent
(help)

stop
hinder
halt
obstruct
impede
preclude
prevention
[see 688]

506

price

cost
charge
fee
expense
outlay
valuation
[see 144]

507

principal
(subordinate)

first
main
leading
chief
foremost
dominant
principally
[see 374]

508

principle

standard
ideal
guideline
theory
ethics
precept

509

prison
(freedom)

jail
gaol
cell
dungeon
captivity
confinement
prisoner
imprison
[see 315]

510

prisoner

captive
jailbird
slave
convict
hostage
detainee
imprisoned

511

prize
(penalty)

reward
gain
honour
cup
medal
trophy
prizewinner
[see 553]

512

probably
(improbably)

likely
doubtless
apparently
supposedly
unquestionably
ostensibly
probability

513

profit
(loss)

gain
earnings
income
interest
benefit
advantage
profitable
[see 244]

514

promise
(deny)

agree
assure
guarantee
swear
pledge
testify

515

proper
(improper)

right
correct
suitable
fitting
decent
appropriate
properly
[see 143]

516

property

goods
belongings
possessions
effects
assets
substance
properties

517

protect
(expose)

guard
defend
shelter
safeguard
secure
preserve
protector
protection
[see 149, 264, 584]

518

proud
(humble)

vain
haughty
arrogant
conceited
pompous
imperious
pride

519

pull
(push)

tug
drag
tow
draw
haul
wrench

520

pupil
(teacher)

learner
scholar
student
beginner
novice
initiate

521

pure
(impure)

real
natural
honest
faultless
genuine
unadulterated
purity
[see 418, 538, 770]

522

purpose

plan
aim
intention

contd.

resolve
project
objective
purposeful
[see 407, 484]

523

push
(pull)

move
press
thrust
ram
force
propel
[see 503]

524

put
(take)

lay
place
set
plant
deposit
impose
putting
[see 340]

525

puzzle
(solution)

problem
mystery
riddle
conundrum
enigma
dilemma
puzzling
[see 136]

526

quantity

amount
measure
size
extent
substance
aggregate
[see 385, 632]

527

quarrel
(agree)

disagree
squabble
argue
dispute
contend
altercate
quarrelling
quarrelsome
[see 138, 220]

528

quick
(slow)

fast
swift
rapid
sudden
instantaneous
expeditious
[see 213, 660, 704, 714]

529

quiet
(noisy)

silent
peaceful
undisturbed
restful
calm
tranquil
quietness
[see 91, 467, 626]

530

quite

fully
totally
completely
exactly
positively
precisely

531

ragged
(smart)

torn
shabby
tattered
threadbare
slovenly
unkempt
[see 492]

532

rain
(drought)

drizzle
shower
downpour
torrent
cloudburst
deluge
rainfall

533

raise
(lower)

pull up
lift
hoist
elevate
lever
erect
raising
[see 351]

534

rare
(common)

few
scarce
uncommon
exceptional
singular
phenomenal
rarely
rarity
[see 586, 659]

535

raw
(cooked)

natural
fresh
uncooked
crude
untried
immature

536

reach

get
grasp
stretch
obtain
extend
attain
[see 251]

537

ready
(reluctant)

prepared
willing
eager
equipped
primed
enthusiastic
readiness
[see 821]

538

real
(false)

true
genuine

contd.

actual
pure
tangible
authentic
reality
[see 521, 770, 772]

539

receive
(give)

get
take
accept
obtain
acquire
inherit
receiving
receipt
reception
[see 251]

540

reduce
(increase)

lessen
shorten
shrink
decrease
diminish
truncate
reducing
reduction
[see 617]

541

referee

judge
umpire
arbitrator
peacemaker
mediator
adjudicator
refereeing
refereed
[see 321, 777]

542

refuse
(accept)

deny
reject
forbid
rebuff
prohibit
disdain
refusal

543

regard
(disregard)

see
look
watch
notice
observe
consider
[see 362, 433, 596, 806]

544

regular
(irregular)

steady
unchanging
punctual
systematic
invariable
consistent
regularity

545

release
(bind)

set free
loosen
untie
liberate
disentangle
extricate
[see 363, 779]

546

remain
(depart)

stay
stop
wait
linger
sojourn
endure
remains
remainder
[see 465, 796]

547

remember
(forget)

recall
recollect
recognise
memorise
reminisce
commemorate
remembrance

548

reply
(ignore)

answer
respond
retort
rejoin

riposte
acknowledge
replied
replying
[see 29]

549

report
(suppression)

news
story
statement
account
disclosure
revelation
[see 673]

550

rescue
(endanger)

save
aid
recover
release
deliver
liberate
rescuing
[see 584]

551

rest
(move)

lie
sleep
repose
recline
relax
retire
restful
[see 349, 636]

552

return
(depart)

reappear
reverse
retreat
rebound
revert
recur

553

reward
(punishment)

payment
award
prize
bonus
recompense

contd.

gratuity
[see 511]

554

rich
(poor)

well-off
wealthy
moneyed
prosperous
affluent
opulent
[see 810]

555

right
(wrong)

correct
true
exact
accurate
valid
unerring
[see 143, 770]

556

ring

toll
chime
peal
clang
resound
reverberate
rang
rung

557

ripe
(unripe)

full
grown
ready
developed
mellow
mature
ripen

558

rise
(fall)

climb
arise
ascend
mount
soar
zoom
rose
risen
[see 118]

559

river

stream
rivulet
tributary
rapids
meander
estuary

560

road

street
lane
avenue
highway
route
motorway
[see 756]

561

roam

wander
stroll
ramble
stray
saunter
meander
[see 800]

562

roar
(whisper)

shout
yell
bellow
bawl
growl
snarl
[see 107, 618, 838]

563

rob
(enrich)

steal
burgle
pilfer
loot
plunder
deprive
robbing
robbed
[see 564, 677, 736]

564

robber
(protector)

thief
burglar
crook
pickpocket
criminal
brigand
robbery
[see 563, 736, 738]

565

rock

pebble
stone
boulder
crag
cliff
outcrop
[see 687]

566

rod

stick
cane
pole
post
shaft
baton
[see 52, 490, 682]

567

roll

turn
bowl
wheel
revolve
trundle
rotate
[see 775]

568

roof

cover
shelter
ceiling
canopy
awning
dome
roofs

569

rough
(smooth)

uneven
rugged
jagged
bristly
coarse
gnarled
roughness

570

round

curved
rounded
spherical

contd.

rotund
circular
convex

571

route

way
path
road
course
march
itinerary
routing
[see 464, 756]

572

row
(quietness)

noise
uproar
brawl
riot
disturbance
commotion
rowdy
[see 366, 428]

573

rub

wipe
clean
smear
polish
massage
burnish
rubbing
rubbed
rubber
[see 824]

574

rude
(polite)

impolite
uncivil
ill-mannered
discourteous
impertinent
brusque
rudeness

575

rule

govern
control
manage
command
regulate
dominate
[see 141]

576

run

rush
hurry
hasten
race
sprint
accelerate
running
runner
[see 577]

577

rush

hurry
dash
scurry
tear
fly
charge
[see 576]

578

sad
(happy)

unhappy
sorry
downcast
depressed
mournful

disconsolate
sadness
saddened
[see 653, 780]

579

safe
(dangerous)

sure
sound
trusty
certain
dependable
reliable
safety

580

sailor

seaman
fisherman
seafarer
mariner
captain
yachtsman

581

same
(different)

alike
similar
matching
equal
duplicate
identical
sameness

582

satisfy
(dissatisfy)

please
content
gratify
gladden
suffice
satiate
satisfied

583

savage
(docile)

wild
fierce
untamed
vicious
ferocious
barbarous
savagery
[see 155, 219, 820]

584

save
(abandon)

keep
rescue
preserve
guard
protect
liberate
saving
[see 264, 517, 550]

585

say

speak
tell
remark
state
mention
relate
said
[see 658, 718, 727]

586

scarce
(plentiful)

rare
few
uncommon
scanty
deficient

contd.

meagre
scarcity
scarcely
[see 534, 659]

587

scare
(reassure)

frighten
alarm
startle
shock
terrify
horrify
scaring
[see 16, 734]

588

scene

view
sight
show
display
spectacle
panorama
scenery
scenic
[see 624, 792]

589

scent
(stench)

smell
odour
perfume
fragrance
aroma
redolence
[see 641]

590

science
(art)

physics
chemistry
biology
astronomy
technology
electronics
scientific

591

scream
(whisper)

cry
yell
screech
shriek
squeal
squawk
[see 90, 156]

592

sea
(land)

ocean
wave
breaker
swell
surge
the deep

593

search

look
seek
hunt
examine
investigate
scrutinise
[see 303, 597]

594

seat

chair
stool

bench
couch
settee
throne
[see 62, 102]

595

secret
(open)

unknown
hidden
unseen
disguised
intimate
confidential
secretive

596

see
(disregard)

look
watch
notice
observe
discern
witness
saw
[see 362, 433, 543, 806]

597

seek
(shun)

look
search
follow
pursue
enquire
explore
sought
[see 303, 593]

598

seldom
(often)

not often
rarely
hardly ever
scarcely
occasionally
infrequently

599

send
(detain)

post
forward
deliver
convey
despatch
transmit
sent

600

sense
(nonsense)

meaning
understanding
reason
sanity
wisdom
sagacity
sensible
[see 825]

601

separate
(join)

divide
part
disconnect
sever
detach
segregate
separation
[see 181, 663]

602

serious
(trivial)

important
momentous
dangerous
significant
consequential
crucial
seriousness
[see 309]

603

serve
(command)

obey
help
aid
assist
attend
perform
service
serving
[see 284, 635, 707]

604

set
(individual)

group
party
band
gang
company
clique
[see 50, 122, 133]

605

settle
(derange)

arrange
fix
decide
determine
resolve
stabilise
settlement

606

shade
(glare)

shadow
darkness
dusk
gloom
dimness
obscurity
shady
[see 161]

607

shake
(stand)

shiver
tremble
shudder
quiver
vibrate
convulse
shaky

608

shape
(shapeless)

form
figure
build
image
pattern
outline
shapely

609

share
(whole)

part
portion
ration
due
allocation
inheritance

sharing
[see 458, 478]

610

sharp
(blunt)

cutting
pointed
jagged
keen
fine
acute
sharpness

611

shelter
(exposure)

cover
screen
protection
safety
shield
refuge
[see 271]

612

shine

glow
gleam
beam
glisten
illuminate
scintillate
shone
shiny
[see 352]

613

ship

boat
craft
steamer
vessel
ferry
liner
[see 69, 760]

614

shoot

fire
hit
propel
project
discharge
emit
shot

615

shop

store
stall
market
department
supermarket
boutique
shopping
shopped
[see 689, 706]

616

shore

beach
coast
seaside
strand
foreshore
seaboard
[see 55, 123]

617

short
(long)

brief
squat
stunted
dwarfish
diminished
abbreviated
[see 540]

618

shout

call
cry
cheer
roar
bellow
yell
[see 107, 562, 838]

619

show
(hide)

display
reveal
exhibit
expose
unveil
demonstrate
shown
[see 454]

620

shut
(open)

close
slam
fasten
lock
bolt
secure
[see 119, 359]

621

shy
(bold)

timid
modest
bashful
cautious
reserved
demure
shyly
[see 424]

622

sick
(well)

ill
unwell
ailing
unhealthy
diseased
indisposed
sickness
[see 177, 308]

623

side
(centre)

edge
border
verge
margin
fringe
flank
[see 195]

624

sight

view
scene
show
exhibition
prospect
spectacle
[see 588, 792]

625

sign

mark
signal
symbol
emblem
token
indication
[see 382]

626

silent
(noisy)

quiet
hushed
noiseless
peaceful
undisturbed
muted
silence
[see 91, 467, 529]

627

silly
(wise)

stupid
foolish
senseless
unwise
absurd
ridiculous
silliness

628

simple
(complex)

easy
plain
clear
natural
understandable
intelligible
simplicity
[see 193]

629

sing

chant
chorus
croon
vocalise
serenade
warble
sang
sung

630

single
(numerous)

alone
solitary
particular
isolated
exclusive
unique
singular
[see 22, 445]

631

sit
(stand)

be seated
rest
straddle
bestride
loll
sprawl
sitting
sat

632

size

measurement
width
extent
magnitude
dimensions
proportions
[see 385, 526]

633

skin
(bone)

covering
hide

contd.

pelt
peel
shell
cortex
skinned

634

skip

jump
spring
dance
frisk
leap
gambol
skipping
skipped
[see 322, 669]

635

slave

captive
serf
vassal
drudge
servant
menial
slavery
slavish
[see 603]

636

sleep
(wake)

slumber
doze
rest
nap
repose
snooze
slept
[see 551, 749]

637

slip

trip
fall
slide
slither
stumble
miscalculate
slipping
slipped
slippery
[see 209, 768]

638

slow
(quick)

late
behind
slack
gradual
sluggish
dilatory
[see 337]

639

small
(large)

little
tiny
miniature
slight
inconsiderable
insignificant
[see 356, 748]

640

smart
(shabby)

neat
trim
tidy
elegant
dapper
fashionable
smartness
[see 422]

641

smell

odour
aroma
scent
stink
stench
fragrance
[see 589]

642

smile
(frown)

grin
laugh
smirk
beam
simper
grimace
smiling
[see 338]

643

smoke

mist
steam
fog
smog
haze
vapour
smoking
smoky

644

smooth
(rough)

flat
level
plane
even
polished
sleek
[see 202, 226, 347]

645

snap

break
crack
bite
nip
fracture
sever
snapping
snapped
snappy
[see 78, 150]

646

soft
(hard)

pliant
yielding
pliable
tender
downy
delicate
soften
[see 729]

647

soil

earth
dirt
ground
loam
mud
sediment
[see 191, 262]

648

solid
(hollow)

hard
firm
dense
thick
compact
impenetrable
solidify
[see 272, 753]

649

sometimes

at times
now and then
now and again
every so often
once in a while
occasionally

650

song

tune
melody
lyric
solo
chorus
serenade
sing
sang
[see 413, 774]

651

soon
(late)

shortly
early
promptly
presently
directly
expeditiously
[see 190]

652

sore
(painless)

hurting
tender
painful
aching
sensitive
inflamed
soreness
[see 451, 685]

653

sorry
(glad)

sad
sorrowful
apologetic
repentant
miserable
sympathetic
sorrow
[see 578, 780]

654

sort
(muddle)

arrange
choose
order
select
classify
categorise
[see 112, 475]

655

sound
(silence)

noise
tone
note
music
clamour
resonance
[see 413, 428, 744]

656

sour
(sweet)

acid
sharp
bitter
tart
rancid
unpalatable
sourness

657

spare

extra
additional

surplus
reserve
unneeded
superfluous
sparing

658

speak

say
talk
tell
declare
address
proclaim
spoke
spoken
[see 585, 718, 727]

659

special

unusual
uncommon
different
rare
particular
exceptional
specially
speciality
[see 459, 534, 586]

660

speed
(slowness)

quickness
swiftness
rate
rapidity
acceleration
velocity
speedy
[see 528]

661

spirit
(lethargy)

life
energy
activity
courage
vigour
enthusiasm
spirited
[see 350]

662

splendid

great
noble
magnificent
glorious
admirable
sublime
splendour
[see 260]

663

split
(unite)

cut
tear
crack
divide
separate
bisect
splitting
[see 181, 601]

664

spoil
(improve)

harm
damage
injure
ruin
destroy
disfigure
spoilt
[see 158]

665

sport

play
game
fun
pleasure
relaxation
recreation
sportsman
[see 245, 486]

666

spot

mark
point
patch
stain
blemish
stigma
spotted
[see 382]

667

sprain

turn
twist
jerk
pull
strain
wrench

668

spread
(contain)

extend
enlarge
broadcast
distribute
circulate
propagate
[see 696, 713]

669

spring

jump
leap
hop
skip
bound
vault
sprang
sprung
[see 322, 634]

670

stand
(move)

stay
stop
halt
rest
remain
endure
stood
[see 675, 676, 688]

671

stare
(glance)

look
gaze
gape
watch
goggle
eye
staring

672

start

begin
commence
originate
establish
introduce
initiate
[see 60]

673

statement

saying
account
announcement
declaration

testimony
evidence
[see 549]

674

station

place
site
location
depot
terminal
destination
[see 483, 496]

675

stationary
(mobile)

still
fixed
motionless
inactive
stable
immobile
[see 670, 684]

676

stay
(go)

stop
wait
linger
delay
remain
pause
[see 670, 793]

677

steal

take
rob
thieve
pilfer
seize
embezzle
stole
stolen
[see 563, 736, 738]

678

steep

sudden
abrupt
sheer
arduous
vertical
precipitous
steepness

679

steer

guide
pilot
direct
conduct
control
navigate
steersman
[see 266, 342, 480]

680

stem

stalk
branch
stock
body
trunk
support

681

step

tread
stride
pace
footfall
walk
gait
[see 798]

682

stick

cane
rod

contd.

staff
pole
club
bludgeon
[see 52, 490, 566]

683

stiff
(pliant)

firm
rigid
unbending
unyielding
resistant
inflexible
stiffness
[see 272]

684

still
(agitated)

unmoving
fixed
motionless
stationary
immobile
inert
stillness
[see 675]

685

sting

pain
hurt
prick
wound
pierce
afflict
stung
[see 451, 652]

686

stock

store
supply
hoard
quantity
reserve
provision
[see 479, 689, 706]

687

stone

pebble
rock
shingle
boulder
slab
monolith
stony
[see 565]

688

stop
(start)

finish
end
halt
cease
discontinue
desist
stopping
stopped
[see 168, 223, 505, 670]

689

store

stock
supply
fund
hoard
abundance
provision
storing
[see 479, 615, 686, 706]

690

storm
(calm)

thunderstorm
hailstorm
squall

cloudburst
blizzard
hurricane

691

story

tale
fable
yarn
novel
narrative
history
stories

692

straight
(crooked)

direct
upright
erect
linear
vertical
perpendicular
[see 202]

693

strange
(ordinary)

odd
unusual
uncommon
peculiar
singular
extraordinary
strangeness
strangely
stranger
[see 441]

694

stream

brook
beck
burn
river
channel
tributary

695

strength
(weakness)

power
force
might
energy
brawn
vitality
strong
strengthen
[see 199, 393, 498, 698]

696

stretch
(shorten)

lengthen
expand
extend
spread
increase
elongate
[see 668, 713]

697

strict
(lenient)

stern
hard
harsh
severe
rigid
stringent
strictness

698

strong
(weak)

powerful
forceful
mighty

contd.

energetic
brawny
robust
strength
[see 279, 393, 498, 695]

699

struggle

fight
wrestle
grapple
try
endeavour
venture
struggling
[see 220]

700

study

learn
read
watch
examine
contemplate
deliberate
studying
studied
studies
[see 343]

701

stuff

cloth
fabric
goods
material
substance
matter

702

subtract
(add)

take
remove
withdraw
deduct
abstract
abridge
subtraction

703

succeed
(fail)

win
prosper
progress
accomplish
achieve
prevail
success
[see 822]

704

sudden
(gradual)

quick
rapid
hurried
unexpected
instant
immediate
suddenness
[see 528]

705

suggest

hint
mention
propose
advise
recommend
advocate
suggestion
[see 12]

706

supply
(demand)

store
stock

hoard
reserve
provision
resource
supplying
supplied
supplies
[see 615, 686, 689]

707

support
(oppose)

help
aid
assist
befriend
strengthen
reinforce
[see 284, 603]

708

suppose

think
believe
fancy
imagine
presume
postulate
supposition
[see 61, 265, 740]

709

sure
(doubtful)

certain
positive
satisfied
convinced
confident
assured
surety
[see 101]

710

surprise

shock
blow
wonder
amazement
astonishment
revelation
surprising
[see 16, 587, 828]

711

sweep

brush
clean
clear
tidy
scour
vacuum
swept
[see 115]

712

sweet
(bitter)

sugary
honied
candied
tasty
delicious
delectable
sweetness
[see 169, 722]

713

swell
(reduce)

fatten
increase
enlarge
expand
inflate
distend
swollen
[see 668, 696]

714

swift
(slow)

fast
quick
rapid
speedy
hurried
expeditious
swiftness
[see 213, 528]

715

swing

hang
sway
dangle
waver
alternate
oscillate
swung
[see 269]

716

system
(chaos)

plan
order
method
scheme
arrangement
organisation
systematic
[see 391, 448, 484, 808]

717

take
(give)

get
grasp
seize
accept
capture
appropriate
taken
took
[see 2, 244, 251, 438]

718

talk

speak
chatter
gossip
mumble
express
articulate
talkative
[see 585, 658, 727]

719

tall
(short)

lanky
long
high
lofty
giant
towering
tallness
[see 286, 361]

720

tame
(wild)

gentle
mild
trained
docile
domesticated
submissive
tameness
[see 249]

721

target

mark
aim
goal
butt

purpose
objective

722

taste

try
flavour
savour
relish
appetite
experience
tasting
tasty
[see 169, 712]

723

tax

payment
toll
duty
levy
tariff
excise

724

teach

tell
show
demonstrate
instruct
inform
enlighten
taught

725

team
(individual)

group
band
party
crew
troupe
company
[see 50, 122, 133, 781]

726

tease

worry
annoy
disturb
torment
provoke
tantalise
teasing
[see 832]

727

tell

describe
explain
inform
report
disclose
divulge
told
[see 585, 658, 718]

728

temper
(calm)

mood
anger
annoyance
irritation
petulance
exasperation
[see 26, 153]

729

tender
(harsh)

kind
mild
gentle
comforting
sympathetic
compassionate
tenderness
[see 249, 328, 646]

730

term

time
period
spell
season
duration
cycle
termly
terminal
[see 472, 747]

731

terrible

awful
shocking
frightful
horrible
gruesome
horrendous
terribly
[see 44, 587]

732

terrific (1)

awful
terrible
dreadful
fearful
frightful
intimidating
terrify
terrified
[see 44]

733

terrific (2)

marvellous
fantastic
exceptional
wonderful
tremendous
sensational
[see 828]

734

terrify

frighten
shock
scare
terrorise
horrify
petrify
terrifying
terrified
[see 587]

735

test

proof
trial
examination
ordeal
investigation
analysis

736

theft

stealing
robbery
burglary
thieving
purloining
larceny
thief
[see 563, 564, 677, 738]

737

thick
(thin)

solid
fat
broad
bulky
dense
gross
thickness
[see 215, 819]

738

thief

robber
burglar
pickpocket
housebreaker
pilferer
kleptomaniac
thieves
thieving
thieved
thievery
[see 564, 677, 736]

739

thin
(thick)

lean
slim
skinny
slender
slight
emaciated
thinner
thinned
thinness
[see 415]

740

think

reason
understand
consider
concentrate
ponder
deliberate
thought
[see 265, 708, 742, 827]

741

thirsty

dry
parched
craving
longing
arid
dehydrated
[see 188]

742

thought

thinking
concern
attention
meditation
deliberation
cogitation
thoughtful
thoughtless
[see 306, 740]

743

throw

cast
pitch
toss
hurl
propel
precipitate
threw
thrown
[see 482]

744

thunder

boom
rumble
crash
roll
resound
reverberate
thunderous
[see 366, 428, 655]

745

tie
(loosen)

fasten
join
bind
connect
attach
secure
tying
tied
[see 214, 225, 318, 782]

746

tight
(loose)

firm
fastened
close
taut
stretched
tense

747

time

day
term
period
interval
interlude
interim
timeless
timely
[see 403, 443, 472, 730]

748

tiny
(huge)

small
little
dwarfish
minute
minuscule
infinitesimal
tiniest
[see 356, 639]

749

tired
(energetic)

weary
spent
worn
drowsy
sleepy
exhausted
tiring
[see 636]

750

tool

gadget
machine
utensil
instrument
implement
device
[see 372]

751

top
(bottom)

tip
point
peak
crest
apex
pinnacle
topmost
topped
[see 468]

752

touch

feel
hold
handle
stroke
contact

manipulate
[see 291]

753

tough
(fragile)

strong
hard
rigid
robust
substantial
durable
toughness
[see 272, 648]

754

tower

turret
belfry
castle
keep
minaret
campanile
[see 98]

755

town
(village)

city
borough
township
settlement
municipality
metropolis
townsman
[see 113]

756

track

way
path
trail
lane
course
route
[see 462, 464, 560, 571]

757

trade

barter
bargaining
business
commerce
exchange
marketing
trading
[see 204]

758

trail

follow
hunt
trace
track
shadow
pursue
[see 104, 230, 303]

759

tramp
(ride)

walk
plod
march
hike
travel
trudge
[see 287, 381, 798]

760

transport

lorry
bus
ship
train
aircraft
conveyance
[see 69, 94, 613]

761

trap

net
snare
pitfall
ambush
ruse
decoy
trapping
trapped
trapper

762

travel
(settle)

move
tour
journey
wander
roam
traverse
travelling
travelled
traveller
[see 319, 794]

763

treasure
(trash)

money
riches
wealth
valuables
jewels
bullion
[see 233, 404]

764

treat
(punishment)

party
picnic
feast
amusement
entertainment
excursion
[see 476]

765

trial

case
hearing
action
suit
enquiry
ordeal

766

tribe

family
clan
race
division
stock
dynasty
tribal

767

trick

joke
prank
hoax
fraud
swindle
deception
trickery
tricky
[see 106]

768

trip

fall
slip
stumble
sprawl
topple
lurch
tripped
[see 209, 637]

769

trouble
(joy)

worry
bother
distress
annoyance
inconvenience
aggravation
troublesome
[see 74, 435]

770

true
(false)

real
correct
exact
genuine
accurate
authentic
truism
truth
[see 143, 521, 538, 555, 772]

771

trust
(mistrust)

belief
hope
faith
reliance
assurance
conviction
trustworthy
[see 61]

772

truth
(falsehood)

fact
reality
honesty
accuracy
certainty
authenticity
truthfulness
[see 207, 538, 770]

773

try
(abandon)

attempt
undertake
aim
venture
strive
endeavour
tried
trial

774

tune

song
melody
air
chant
carol
harmony
tuneful
[see 413, 650]

775

turn

spin
reverse
revolve
pivot
rotate
gyrate
[see 567]

776

ugly
(beautiful)

plain
unattractive
ungainly
hideous
repulsive
loathsome
ugliness

777

umpire

judge
referee
peacemaker
mediator
intermediary
arbitrator
umpiring
[see 321, 541]

778

understand
(misapprehend)

know
learn
comprehend
assume
surmise
deduce
understood
[see 330, 343]

779

undo
(tie)

untie
unfasten
unhook
unlace
loosen
unshackle
undone
[see 363, 545]

780

unhappy
(happy)

sad
glum
miserable
sorrowful
downcast
inconsolable
unhappiness
unhappily
[see 578, 653]

781

union

company
society
group
league
guild
brotherhood
[see 50, 725]

782

unite
(separate)

join
connect
bind
combine
co-operate
amalgamate
unity
[see 318, 745]

783

upset

spill
topple
overturn
overbalance
capsize
invert
upsetting

784

use

handle
operate
exercise
employ
utilise

manipulate
useful
useless
[see 785]

785

useful
(useless)

helpful
handy
convenient
worthwhile
effective
utilitarian
usefulness
[see 784]

786

usual
(exceptional)

ordinary
common
familiar
normal
typical
unremarkable
usually
[see 132]

787

vacant
(occupied)

empty
unoccupied
abandoned
uninhabited
deserted
void
vacancy
vacancies
[see 68, 196]

788

valuable
(worthless)

costly
expensive
rare
special
precious
priceless
value
[see 833]

789

various

several
many
different
assorted
dissimilar
variegated
[see 379]

790

vehicle

coach
carriage
wagon
automobile
conveyance
transporter
[see 94]

791

very
(slightly)

quite
highly
remarkably
extremely
exceedingly
unequivocally

792

view

sight
scene

contd.

landscape
prospect
vista
panorama
[see 588, 624]

793

visit

call
stop
stay
appear
sojourn
commune
visitor
[see 676]

794

voyage

trip
sail
cruise
passage
journey
expedition
voyager
[see 319, 762]

795

wages

pay
earnings
hire
payment
salary
emolument
[see 466]

796

wait
(depart)

stop
stay
linger
delay
remain
postpone
[see 465, 546]

797

wake
(sleep)

move
waken
awake
arouse
enliven
animate
[see 42]

798

walk

stroll
march
stride
hike
ramble
saunter
[see 287, 381, 681, 759]

799

wall

fence
partition
divider
screen
separator
bulkhead

800

wander
(settle)

roam
stray
ramble
rove
range
meander
wanderlust
[see 561]

801

want
(possess)

wish
need
crave
require
desire
covet
[see 423, 492, 826]

802

war
(peace)

fighting
battle
combat
warfare
hostilities
massacre
warlike
[see 54, 138, 220]

803

warm
(cool)

heated
tepid
hot
lukewarm
snug
comfortable
warmth
[see 130, 282, 300]

804

wash
(soil)

clean
bathe
scrub
shampoo
cleanse
launder
[see 115]

805

waste
(preserve)

spend
consume
misuse
squander
improverish
dissipate
wastrel

806

watch
(disregard)

see
notice
observe
guard
contemplate
survey
watchful
[see 362, 433, 543, 596]

807

wave

signal
shake
beckon
brandish
flutter
flourish
waving
wavy

808

way

manner
plan
method
scheme
system
process
[see 391, 484, 716]

809

weak
(strong)

feeble
frail
fragile
delicate
unsound
powerless
weakness

810

wealth
(poverty)

riches
possessions
property
capital
affluence
opulence
[see 554]

811

wear

put on
bear
carry
don
display
exhibit
wore
worn

812

welcome
(deter)

greet
meet
salute
hail
receive
address
[see 386]

813

well
(ill)

healthy
hearty
sound
robust
hale
vigorous
[see 279]

814

wet
(dry)

watery
soaked
drenched
moist
humid
saturated
wetness
wetter
[see 159]

815

whip

lash
flog
thrash
chastise
scourge
castigate
whipping
whipped
[see 56, 289]

816

whisper
(shout)

murmur
breathe
sigh
mutter
mumble
sibilate

817

white
(black)

light
pale
pallid
snowy
chalk-white
snow-white
[see 452]

818

wicked
(virtuous)

bad
evil
sinful
odious
villainous
infamous
wickedness
[see 47, 416]

819

wide
(narrow)

broad
thick
outspread
expansive
spacious
extensive
width
[see 737]

820

wild
(tame)

savage
fierce
ferocious
untamed
barbarous
undomesticated
wildness
[see 219, 583]

821

willing
(loath)

ready
prepared
eager
agreeable
co-operative
amenable
willingness
[see 537]

822

win
(lose)

gain
succeed
triumph
achieve
accomplish
procure
winner
winning
won
[see 703]

823

wind

breath
draught
breeze
gust
gale
hurricane

824

wipe

rub
clean
dry
stroke

contd.

scour
smear
wiping
[see 573]

825

wise
(foolish)

sensible
intelligent
cautious
shrewd
sagacious
sapient
wisdom
[see 600]

826

wish
(spurn)

want
choose
desire
hunger
crave
yearn
wishful
[see 423, 801]

827

wonder

think
ponder
question
meditate
speculate
conjecture
[see 265, 740]

828

wonderful

surprising
amazing
remarkable
extraordinary
astonishing
miraculous
wondrous
wonderfully
[see 470, 710, 733]

829

wood

woodland
thicket
forest
copse
grove
coppice

830

word

name
sign
symbol
term
expression
ideogram
wordiness
[see 334]

831

work
(play)

labour
task
toil
employment
exertion
industry
[see 317, 331, 440, 497]

832

worry

annoy
vex
irritate
pester
distress

torment
worried
[see 726]

833

worth

cost
value
merit
quality
importance
perfection
worthy
[see 788]

834

wound

hurt
injury
blow
damage
abrasion
lesion
[see 273, 305]

835

wrap
(unfold)

cover
cloak
muffle
enfold
swathe
encase
wrapping
wrapped
[see 149, 285]

836

write

inscribe
jot
scribble
compose
correspond
communicate
written
wrote

837

wrong
(right)

false
mistaken
incorrect
inaccurate
inexact
unsound

838

yell
(whisper)

shout
scream
cry
bellow
bawl
shriek
[see 562, 618]

839

young
(old)

youthful
childish
innocent
budding
juvenile
immature
youngster
[see 110]

840

zone

area
place
district
region
locality

contd.

territory
zonal
[see 31, 147, 179]

841

zoo

park
safari
menagerie
circus
zoological gardens
zoological park

INDEX

Numbers refer to sections of the thesaurus, not pages. Words in bold type appear as the main words in the text; the appropriate section number is also shown in bold.